I Can Help

by Lynne Rickards

Institute of Education

I can help in the garden.

I can help in the market.

I can help in the barn.

I can help in the shop.

I can help in the kitchen.

I can help in the classroom.

I can help in the library.

RETURNS

I Can Help ~ Lynne Rickards

Teaching notes written by Sue Bodman and Glen Franklin

Using this book

Developing reading comprehension

This non-chronological report uses a simple sentence structure to report on a variety of ways in which children across the world can help. Some of the names of the locations pictured are multisyllabic words (for example, *'library'*, *'classroom'*, *'kitchen'*). This presents a challenge to the young reader who may expect there to be a space between each syllable. Monitoring one-to-one correspondence is key to the effective use of this simple text.

Grammar and sentence structure

- Text is well-spaced to support the development of one-to-one correspondence.
- One line of text and highly predictable changes in the noun supported by clear illustrations.
- In contexts where children are learning English as an additional language, support by rehearsing the sentence structure orally before introducing the book.

Word meaning and spelling

- Use initial letter information to monitor reading (*'garden'*, *'market'*, *'barn'*, *'shop'*, *'kitchen'*, *'classroom'*, *'library'*).
- Reinforce recognition of frequently occurring words *'I'*, *'can'*, *'help'*, *'in'*, *'the'*

Curriculum links

PSHE – The book shows some ways that children can help. *How do children in this class help? How do they help other children? How do they help adults?* Discussion of ways the children can help other people could be followed by illustrating some of the ways that the class help others.

Language development – Using pictures, develop vocabulary of everyday situations. For example, rooms in the home, places we visit, such as library, supermarket, bakery, park. For each place, discuss some ways in which we might help other people.

Learning Outcomes

Children can:

- understand that print carries meaning and is read from left to right
- use initial letter information to check understanding of picture information
- track one line of simple repetitive text.

A guided reading lesson

Book Introduction

Give a book to each child and read the title. Ask the children to point to the title and read it.

Orientation

Give a brief orientation to the text: *The children in this book are all helping. Let's look and see what they do to help.*

Preparation

Page 2: Say: *The girl says 'I can help in the garden.'* Read the text slowly enough for the children to point to each word carefully in their copy as you read. Repeat and support if necessary.

Say: *Well done. Make sure you point carefully when you read by yourself.*

Page 2: Draw attention to the change in location on each page by asking children to check the picture and locate the word that looks right. *This girl is helping in the garden. Find the word 'garden'. That's right. I can hear /g/. That word looks right. Does it make sense with the picture? Yes, it does.*

Turn through pages 6 to 15, making sure that the naming vocabulary is familiar to the children. Make links between the initial letter information and the item in the illustration, as in the example above.